I0480830

Build Your Business in Seven Simple Steps Workbook

Wordran Naa Wilson

CONTENTS

NOTE

Now that you have read the *How to Build a Business in Seven Simple Steps* book, it is recommended that you complete these exercises after you have read the corresponding chapter in the book.

The end of each chapter comes with a blank page for additional notes, so go ahead and record your answers to help you clarify your goals.

If you haven't read the main book already, visit Amazon and search 'Wordran'.

Or scan QR code below.

CHAPTER I.
INCEPTION / IDEA

The main book 'How to Build a Business in 7 Simple Steps' will help you complete exercises in this workbook.

WHAT TYPE OF BUSINESS SHOULD I START?

There is never 100% certainty your business idea will be a success; however, by exploring your motivations and understanding the value that you can give (and receive), you'll develop confidence in your business idea.

Exercise 1

Understanding the fundamentals of why you want to be in business is the foundation of creating a successful business. With greater clarity about your 'whys', the easier it is to define your business's mission and authentically connect with your target audience. Exploring your 'whys' also helps you to develop your 'hows'.

Going up against competitors, you really want to be memorable and magnetic to your audience.

Go ahead, answer the questions below. Write down as much as you can; remember, this is what makes you tick, your motivations. It's highly subjective and there is no wrong or right. As you reflect, you may change some of the detail – go with it!

Why do you want to start your own business? *Is there an emotional reason behind your WHY?*	What problem does your WHY solve/address?

Exercise 2

You know what you want to take to the world, so now you need to dig deeper. This exercise helps you to gain clarity to the direction to take your business idea in.

Passion	List below
To keep motivated and inspired in business, you need to love it! If you don't have **joy** in your work, business is a **chore**. You will have several interests, skills, and capabilities, but what aspect of your business idea are you passionate about? *Perhaps the potential for financial reward excites you, helping people to make a positive change to their lives; or enhancing your professional reputation?* What will give you the **most joy**?	
Knowledge	List below
Be realistic about the knowledge. The key to success is being aware of your strengths and weaknesses. What area of the business and/or industry are you most knowledgeable about? What transferable skills do you possess? Where do your talents lie?	

Profit	List below
Where are you going to make the most profit from your business idea? You must understand where to focus your energy to maximise the opportunities you have. Complete the break-even analysis to test your profitability	

Exercise 3

Break-even analysis helps you to determine the point at which the total cost of providing your product or service and the total revenue are equal. I call it the 'enough' point – if there is no loss or gain, you have broken even.

To test the profitability of your venture, visit www.atbba.co.uk/services/startup-corner. Anything above the enough point is your profit, and anything below is a loss.

Exercise 4

You can be an expert in your field and passionate about meeting the needs of clients and customers, but if there is little profit in your current business idea, your business will not thrive.

Similarly, if you are going into business purely to make a profit, you risk burn out and potentially damaging your commercial reputation. For a successful and sustainable business, there needs to be balance between passion, knowledge, and profit.

Having completed Exercise 1, you now have greater clarity about your strengths and motivations, your skills and knowledge, and where you can make money.

This exercise is the opportunity to assess your business idea in a visual way. Where would you place your business idea in the triangle?

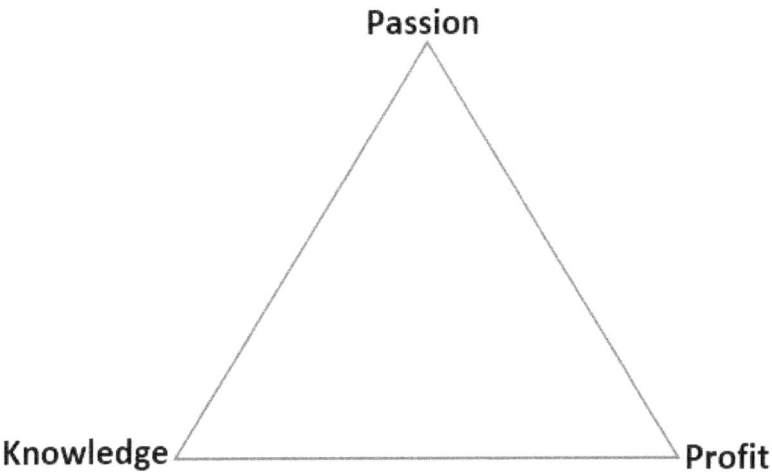

The ideal business is positioned in the centre of the triangle where there is balance between all three headings – you have a passion and the knowledge to make a profit.

Use this page for additional notes

CHAPTER II.
ROADMAP

"Give me six hours to chop down a tree and I will spend the first four sharpening the axe."

– Abraham Lincoln

A strategic road map is one of the best tools for keeping your business on track. As your business evolves, you can tweak it to respond to the business climate and market changes.

Exercise 1

Your road map relies on key information. This exercise helps you to visualise and document the bigger picture of your business.

Answer these questions to help you define your business roadmap:

What are your business' values, and how do they align with your vision? *Values are the fundamental beliefs upon which your business and its behaviours are based.*	
What are your business' values, and how do they align with your vision? *Values are the fundamental beliefs upon which your business and its behaviours are based*	

Identify and document the critical goals and the steps you need to take to achieve them. *Remember, this is high level; you don't need to worry about the finer details right now.*	

Exercise 2

Document your business-critical goals and identify the steps you need to take to achieve them. Remember, this is high level; you don't need to worry about the finer details right now.

	Goals	Objectives/ Steps to take
12 months	*E.g. hire your first employee, reduce ongoing business expenses by 10%, create a new product.*	
Year 3		

Year 5		

Exercise 3

A SWOT analysis helps you to see the positives and negatives of your business. While this is a simple exercise, it is **powerful**. It helps to identify potential challenges and the strategies needed to overcome them, and helps to focus your mind on the opportunities that are available to you.

Strengths: What will give your business the advantage over the competition?

Weaknesses: What areas or characteristics of your business could be disadvantageous or harmful relative to the competition?

Opportunities: What areas in the market can you exploit to help your business grow?

Threats: What aspects of the market could threaten the success of your business?

INTERNAL

Strengths	Weaknesses
E.g. technical expertise, good networking contacts, or high traffic location.	*E.g. single location means limited reach, high startup costs, or dependent on one supplier.*
Opportunities	Threats
E.g. optimise social media channels, underserved communities identified, or press and media coverage.	*E.g. change in government regulations, scarcity of materials, or new competition.*

POSITIVE

NEGATIVE

EXTERNAL

Exercise 4

The power of a SWOT analysis lies in how you interpret it.

Look at the **strengths** you have listed.

- How can you use them to take advantage of the opportunities you have identified?

- How can you use them to overcome the threats/challenges you have listed?

Produce a list of actions to take. Identify where there is a potential skill gap in your business. By being aware of the skill gaps in your business, you can explore outsourcing skills to exploit the opportunities and combat the threats.

	Skill Gap	Actions
Opportunities *E.g. increase sales through your website.*	*E.g. writing skills to target new audiences via the website and social media platforms.*	*E.g. hire a copywriter and/ or digital agency.*

| Threats

E.g. competitors being more up to date with industry innovations.	E.g. lack of experience and knowledge of emerging technologies.	E.g. complete an industry recognised course.

Repeat this exercise for the **weaknesses** you have listed.

- How can the weaknesses limit the opportunities you have identified?

- How can the weaknesses further the risk of experiencing the listed threats/challenges?

	Skill Gap	Actions
Opportunities *E.g. make more sales through cross selling and upselling products.*	*E.g. limited product options.*	*E.g. identify new suppliers with more favourable payment terms.*
Threats *E.g. chaotic and inefficient office processes and procedures.*	*E.g. lack of organisational skills.*	*E.g. attend workshops that focus on back office operations, or automate procedures (accounts, invoices, etc).*

Use this page for additional notes

CHAPTER III.
BUSINESS PLAN

Investing time to plan your business is the wisest investment you can make, and it will give you the greatest returns.

A business plan communicates the roadmap in a formal way and is a tool to attract talent and investors. Most investors and all financial institutions require a business plan. They need to see whether your product/service is fit for market and how you are going to grow and develop your business.

Exercise 1.

This exercise helps you to articulate the primary business goal in a mission statement.

A mission statement is action and outcome-orientated and can be used to inspire consumers and give the business direction.

It's tricky and it takes time, so don't worry if you are finding it hard – it is!

Here are some examples to inspire you:

Company	Mission Statement
Uber	We ignite opportunity by setting the world in motion.
Google	To organize the world's information and make it universally accessible and useful.
Squarespace	Squarespace empowers people with creative ideas to succeed
Business Build Advisory	To teach and empower business owners to develop the skills and confidence to run a sustainable and successful business.

The examples above are written with the consumer as the focus and give clear outcomes for their users.

Answer the following questions:

What is the core activity of your business?	
How do you do it?	
Who does your business serve?	
What makes you different from your competitors?	

The mission statement must align with the voice of your brand and be concise, outcome-oriented, and inclusive. Review your answers and identify the primary elements of each. Underline the standout words you have used and use them as the foundation for your mission statement.

Mission statement:

Exercise 2

A well-written company profile is a document that can be used beyond the business plan. It is a valuable marketing tool to attract clients and customers as well as investors. It's ideal to use on your website, for example, as an 'About Us' page.

Fill in the table below to create a checklist of information you need to include:

		Tick when complete
Company name (the official name that you use for trading)		
Type of business Sole proprietorship/ partnership/ LLC etc		
Ownership Names of key players in your business		
Location Where you are based and the areas you serve		
Company history When and why was the business started? Your 'whys'		

(see Chapter 1: Exercise 1)		
Mission statement (see previous exercise)		
Products/services and target audience An overview of what you sell and to whom		
Objectives An outline of what you want to achieve in the near future, and future growth goals		
Vision statement (see Chapter 2: Exercise 1)		

Use this information to craft a company profile.

Write in the active voice to strengthen the message. Avoid jargon and complex language.

The active voice creates more of an impact. The active voice is when the subject of a sentence performs the verb; the passive voice is when the subject is acted on by the verb.

Active voice	Passive voice
Customers adore our coffee.	Our coffee is adored by customers.

Here are some examples to inspire you:

Company	Company profiles
Starbucks	www.starbucks.com/about-us/company-information
Seattle Cider Company	www.seattlecidercompany.com
Zappos	www.zappos.com/about
Business Build Advisory	atbba.co.uk/about-us

Company profile:

Exercise 3

Business administration is perhaps the least exciting part of running your own business. However, it is crucial to develop good habits. The data you have access to in your business can be used to measure your business success, but what data is needed?

This exercise helps you to determine the key performance indicators (KPIs) for your business. These are high-level metrics, and important for you to understand at the start of your business journey. It's a great way to sharpen your business' administration efficiency.

Refer to the goals you set in Chapter 2: Exercise 1. Write them in the table below and identify which metrics need to be tracked and note the processes you need to implement to capture and save this information.

Goal	Metrics Needed	How
E.g. to increase profit rather than revenue.	*E.g.* 1. *Gross profit* 2. *Sales revenue*	*E.g. to calculate your business's profit margin:* *multiply your gross profit by 100; divide it with your sales.* *If the profit margin increases over time, continue with your strategy. If the figure decreases, you need to cut costs/make your business more efficient.*

Use this page additional notes

CHAPTER IV.
MARKETING STRATEGIES TO GROW YOUR BUSINESS

Market to who really matters

Every business relies on their customers. For business success, a deep understanding of who your ideal client is (beyond a generic demographic description) is needed. Focusing on your ideal client will help you attract them!

This exercise takes you into the mindset of your ideal customer and gives clarity to your marketing.

Answer the following Know Your Customer (KYC) checklist:

Is your ideal customer male of female?	
Do they have family??	
What core values do they have?	
What's their job?	
What's their salary?	
What do they like and dislike about their job?	

What problem can you help them with?	
How important is this issue to them?	
What are the consequences if they don't make changes?	
What are the benefits if they do make changes?	
Have they tried to make changes before? And why did they fail?	
What excuses do they make not to change?	
Why is your business different to the way they have previously tried to address the issue?	

Why does your product/service work better for them?	
What impact will your product/service have for them?	
What is happening in their lives right now that spurs them to take action?	
Do you know where to find them? Social media channels or emailing or visiting businesses?	
Do you have the channels to market to them?	
Have you created a tailor-made marketing materials to reach them?	

Use this page to draw out marketing plan to reach your defined customers

CHAPTER V.
FINANCING YOUR STARTUP

Most business owners haven't got a lot of money to fund their first business idea – they scrape together whatever they possibly can to hit the ground running.

How much money will it take to start your small business?

Calculate the start-up costs for your small business so you can apply for funding, attract investors, and determine when you'll turn a profit.

To create a full financial picture, visit
https://atbba.co.uk/services/startup-corner/

CHAPTER VI.
CHOOSING THE BEST LEGAL STRUCTURE FOR YOUR BUSINESS

Determine which structure provides what benefit for your business.

Choosing the legal structure for your business is an important decision. There are many different variables for you to consider.

Before you take professional advice, refer to your answer to Chapter 2: Exercise 1. What's your long-term vision for the business? Use this exercise to further explore your future business' structure.

Answer the following questions:

How many people will have ownership of your company?	
Will any shareholders benefit financially (other than salary) from the business?	
Will any owners or shareholders be employees of the business (receive payroll benefits)?	
Will you seek a loan from a bank to fund your business?	

Do you have personal assets that you need to protect?	
Is your business vulnerable to lawsuits?	

Use this page additional notes

CHAPTER VII.
PERSONAL DEVELOPMENT

Did you know as a small business, your Unique Sales Point is You?

Personal and professional development is a lifelong process. To thrive professionally, your personal needs must be met too – they are intrinsically linked. Self-awareness and business success go hand-in-hand and are crucial to gain the competitive advantage.

Cultivating personal healthy habits can positively impact your business. Think: exercise for managing stress, eating healthily to maintain productivity, time management to increase efficiency, etc. Learning new skills is an effective way to exercise your brain and boost creativity.

Exercise 1

Use this space to brainstorm goals and values that you would like to focus on for the next 12 months. Perhaps you identified a skill gap in the earlier SWOT analysis exercise you would like to address with an online course? Or perhaps you lack confidence and would benefit from coaching to boost your self-belief?

Exercise 2

Choose one or two goals from the brainstorming that stand out to you.

Fill in the table to create a personal development plan. This provides a framework for you to work within to motivate and give you direction:

	Goal 1:
Benefits I will gain	
Challenges I may face	
Tactics to overcome challenges	
Objectives	
Timeframe	
Resources	
Metrics	

	Goal 2:
Benefits I will gain	
Objectives	
Challenges I may face	
Tactics to overcome challenges	
Timeframe	
Resources	
Metrics